GIRL
TALK

How to survive

ONLINE
EMBARRASSMENT

Lisa Miles and Xanna Eve Chown

rosen publishing's
rosen
central®

NEW YORK

This edition published in 2014 by:

The Rosen Publishing Group, Inc.
29 East 21st Street, New York, NY 10010

Designer: Jeni Child
Editor: Joe Harris
Consultants: Gill Lynas and Emma Hughes
Picture research: Lisa Miles and Xanna Eve Chown
With thanks to Bethany Miller
Picture credits:
All images: Shutterstock

Library of Congress Cataloging-in-Publication Data

Miles, Lisa
How to survive online embarrassment/[Lisa Miles and Xanna Eve Chown].—1st ed.—
New York: Rosen, c2014
        p. cm.—(Girl talk)
Includes index.
ISBN: 978-1-4777-0708-1 (Library Binding)
ISBN: 978-1-4777-0723-4 (Paperback)
ISBN: 978-1-4777-0726-5 (6-pack)
1. Online etiquette—Juvenile literature. 2. Internet—Moral and ethical aspects—Juvenile literature. 3. Internet—Safety measures—Juvenile literature. I. Chown, Xanna Eve. II. Title.
TK5105.878 .M55 2014
303.48'33

Manufactured in China

CPSIA Compliance Information: Batch #S13YA: For further information, contact Rosen Publishing, New York, New York, at 1-800-237-9932.

Contents

computers

The Internet is such a big part of modern life that it's hard to imagine what the world was like without it. We have instant access to a huge amount of information at home, at school, and out and about on our phones.

Did you know?

* In the 1950s, a single computer was big enough to fill a whole room.

* The World Wide Web was invented in 1989.

* The first Web page went live in 1991. It was dedicated to information on the World Wide Web project and was made by Tim Berners-Lee.

* By the year 2000, approxifriendly 50% of people in the USA had Internet access at home – although many thought it was a waste of money and couldn't see what it could be used for.

* Today, we use the Internet for browsing, joining forums, social networking, instant messaging, online video games, shopping, watching videos and TV... and much more!

THEN... AND NOW!

Our newfangled "camera" will make a record of this moment!

Wow, the photos of the party look great!

TOP FIVE... Internet jargon busters

1 **Browser** – this is the program on your computer that you use to visit Web sites.

2 **IP address** – this stands for "Internet Protocol" and it is a number given to a device connected to the Internet. An IP address can be used to identify the country, county, and city from which a computer is connecting to the Internet.

3 **Cookie** – this is a small file stored by your Web browser. It records your Web preferences, such as the language you want your results in.

4 **Malware** – this is software that has been designed to damage a computer system, such as a virus.

5 **Phishing** – this is online fraud that tries to trick you into revealing your username, password, or credit card details, for example by pretending to be your bank.

Netiquette for newbies

Stories from my life

You will NEVER guess what I got for my birthday! Only my own laptop! And it's totally the one I wanted, the right color and really small. Now I don't have to share the computer with my brother anymore – which is a relief because he spends ages on it doing his homework every night and mom lets him. Because, it's "homework."

My mom says there are rules, like I can't use it too late in the evening, and I have to make sure I spend time doing other things, not just chatting on Facebook every night. But that's fine! I am so excited I don't care.

I took a photo of me kissing the keyboard and posted it on Facebook. About thirty seconds later, I got 23 likes and a comment from Sophie saying, "I'm so jealous! I thought I was your one true love!" She really makes me laugh!

I've finally got my own laptop - yay!

Keeping it real:

Where to surf

If you don't have access to a computer at home, there are lots of other ways to get online. For example:

- ✔ School
- ✔ Internet café
- ✔ Youth club
- ✔ Smartphone
- ✔ Public library
- ✔ Community centers/YMCAs

If you are using a shared computer, you should never tick the "remember my ID" or "remember my password" options – and always remember to sign out completely when you have finished your session.

THE rules

There are a lot of strange words associated with the Internet. One of them is netiquette! This means Internet etiquette – or how to treat others online. Just like you always say "thank you" if someone does you a favor, there are things you can do that make being online a better place for everyone.

Help newbies!

Everyone was a new user once. If someone doesn't understand what's going on, it's kind to share your knowledge with them.

* Don't use capitals when you are writing. IT WILL LOOK LIKE YOU ARE SHOUTING! If you want to emphasize a word, you can use *stars.*

* Remember that subtle emotions don't work very well when they are written down. This can lead to misunderstandings. You could think you're being funny, but your friend could think you are being rude. This is why people often use :) or : (to show what emotion they mean.

If someone sends you an important message, it is polite to send them a reply so they know you got it – even if you just say that you'll make a decision or send a longer message later.

Respect other people's copyright. If you use a picture or text from someone else online, make sure you seek and obtain permission and give them a credit.

Don't forward spam (see page 25). People will get annoyed.

Treat others as you would like to be treated yourself. Harassing and insulting other people online is not fair.

I just LOL'd at my best friend's boyfriend. Is that OK?

GIRL TALK

Real-life advice

These rules are very important. Remember, whatever you say online will always be there. Putting nasty comments online can really hurt someone, so just think – is it really worth it?

SOCIAL networking

Did you know there are over 6 million Facebook users — and counting! Facebook is great for keeping in touch, playing games, sharing photos, and a hundred other things. But there are some important things you need to know.

Facebook friends?

It's easy to make friends on Facebook. One click and it's done — as long as the other person agrees! But who should you make friends with? It's a good idea to pick only people you really know — or people you know through good friends. This is because you should only share information with people you know and trust. The last thing you want is your information being used or made fun of by strangers.

✳ Don't forget you can unfriend people if you don't like what they post or feel uncomfortable about being their friend. They won't be alerted to the change. But be careful — you could hurt a real friend if you unfriend them over something silly.

TALKING Point

Have you ever unfriended someone on Facebook? What made you do it?

Mom updates her profile – with a bit of help!

All about you
Family and friends

What should you do if your parents want to be your friends on a social networking site, but you don't want them seeing all your posts? Simple answer: you're going to have to talk it through with them. Try explaining that you are not trying to hide anything, but that it is important to you to have a private life, and you need to be able to talk about your feelings with your friends privately.

EASY Tweeting

Twitter is one of the fastest and easiest ways to get your messages out there. If you want to share a thought, why wait? You can tweet it on the go from your smartphone!

You can tweet from (almost) anywhere!

Keep tweets sweet

Tweets have a maximom length of 140 characters. They can be a fun way to give the people who follow you snapshots of your thoughts. However, Twitter is searchable on Google, so don't ever think that only your followers can read your posts! Every message you send goes out to the whole world, unless you send a direct message to someone to make it private. You can do this by putting DM in front of someone's twitter username when you send your message.

THE LOW DOWN

People use the hashtag symbol # before keywords or phrases to help them show more easily in Twitter Search. If you click on a hashtagged word, you will see all the other tweets that are marked with it.

What's with the hashtag?

Hashtagged words that become very popular are often called trending topics. People often use them to let you know what they're thinking, or as a joke. #funny? #annoying? #youdecide!

TOP FIVE... things NOT to do on Twitter

1. Tweet about absolutely EVERYTHING you do – the world doesn't need to know that much.

2. Apologize for not tweeting for a while – nobody is waiting desperately for your tweets.

3. Spread rumors. Anything you say is likely to get back to the person you're talking about.

4. Post anything that you wouldn't want your mom/ grandmother/the world to read.

5. Post offensive comments – it's just wrong.

I'm really loving my sister's cooking tonight! #notreallylovingit #popcornfordinneragain

HOW TO SAY sorry ...

We've all done it: said or done something that upset somebody else, even if we didn't mean to. But when the mistake happens online, how do you make up for what you've done?

Take it down

✳ The first rule is never to post anything online that you don't want the world to see. But if you do post something you regret, then take it down right away. There are options on all social networking sites for removing material. Find out where they are – and use them if you need to.

✳ The next step is to apologize. Don't just hope that nobody saw – because someone is bound to have seen it. Speak or send a private message to the person who is likely to have been offended. Just say that you're sorry but you posted something stupid online. Tell them that you've taken it down and promise that it won't happen again.

"Sorry" seems to be the hardest word. Oh, and "antidisestablishmentarianism."

I'm sorry I bought the same bag as you, but it looked so good in your profile picture.

All about you — Are your parents on your case?

You probably think you're too old to have your parents keeping an eye on you, right? But try thinking about it from their point of view. They are responsible for your safety – which means making sure that you don't get hurt by anything you see or anything you get involved in, whether that's online or offline.

Talk to them about it – you might be able to reach a compromise. Just say, "Can we talk about what I do when I go online?" and then explain whom you chat with, what games you play, and so on. They might not understand what it is you're doing online, which would make them more worried than they need to be.

TALKING Point

Have YOU ever offended anyone online? What did you do about it?

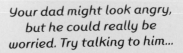

Your dad might look angry, but he could really be worried. Try talking to him...

INTERNET acronyms

An acronym is a word made up of the first letters of a phrase, for example LOL – which stands for Laughing Out Loud. How well do you know your Internet acronyms? Take the test and find out! Give yourself one point for each answer you get right.

ACRONYMS

1. **YOLO**
2. **BRB**
3. **WYCM**
4. **IDK**
5. **ROFL**
6. **IMHO**
7. **FTW**
8. **NSFW**
9. **LMA**
10. **TMI**

BRB

1-6 points

You might want to learn some more Internet acronyms. After all, it's good to know what other people are talking about online.

7-11 points

Not bad! You know what's what, but you're not too much of a geek either! Not that it's bad to be a geek, BTW.

12-15 points

You're really in the know when it comes to techno-talk. How much time do you spend on the Internet? Remember, your friends might prefer a real hug.

11. **BTW**
12. **ILY**
13. **J/K**
14. **XOXO**
15. **THX**

ILY!!!

ANSWERS

*This warns you that the message will contain offensive or inappropriate content.

1. You only live once
2. Be right back
3. Will you call me?
4. I don't know
5. Rolling on the floor laughing
6. In my honest opinion
7. For the win!
8. Not safe for work*
9. Leave me alone
10. Too much information
11. By the way
12. I love you
13. Just kidding
14. Hugs and kisses
15. Thanks

Cyber survival

Stories from my life

I went to Sophie's house and took my new laptop with me. It was so great. We spent ages using the camera to take photos of ourselves wearing hideous clothes, then edited and manipulated them. There was one where our faces looked really squashed and one where our teeth looked really big. SO gross! I was glad no one else saw them…

We went down to the kitchen to get some snacks and left my computer upstairs. But while we were eating, Sophie got a message on her phone, telling her to check out Facebook. OMG.

Sophie's brother had used my computer to get on my Facebook page. He changed my profile pic to one of me with big teeth, and made my status say that I was in love with myself and spent all my time looking in the mirror! Ground, please swallow me up now.

I'll never live this down. I'm going to have to move to a new town. Or country.

TOP FIVE... most annoying status updates

1. *What you had for lunch – "Tuna salad today! Yum!"*

2. *An unsubtle hint about your feelings to make people ask how you're doing – "What a lousy day. Some people are just not good friends."*

3. *Attention seeking – "OMG! All the teachers have it in for me today! I HATE my life!!!"*

4. *Fishing for compliments – "It's nearly vacation time, and I'm SO not ready for my bikini!"*

5. *Saying how great your boyfriend is – "Davey U R so cute! Love U baby!"*

Try to avoid posting too many pictures of you pouting at the camera!

All about you
How to deal with embarrassment

* If someone else's post embarrasses you, what should you do? If you decide to post a response, keep it as short and friendly as possible. Adding too much extra information could make it worse.

* Try to laugh about it. If you say, "I meant to do that!" with a smile, people may start to laugh with you instead of at you.

* Remember that in time whatever it is won't seem so awful. You might even manage to laugh about it!

OMG!
IT SAYS WHAT?

What kind of things do you post on social media sites? How you're feeling today? The latest jokes? Or gossip that somebody told you at a party? Er... you might want to think about that last one.

Do you think before you post?

It's great to share... but what if the info or the image isn't yours? It's a good idea to think for a moment before you post anything online. For instance, if your sister told you that she's getting engaged, don't leap straight onto Facebook. Because then your friends will know before her friends, and your sister will be heartbroken that she didn't get to share her news.

The same goes for photos. If you took a silly picture of your friend doing a ridiculous dance at a party, she might not think it's so funny when you post it online. Show her first – she might share the joke, or she might prefer that her crush (and the world) DOESN'T get to see it!

Apparently I'm engaged – to someone called Melvin?!

Keeping it real:

What **NOT** to post

 Your personal details, such as your address, your date of birth, or your phone number. Some people use personal information for illegal activities, so don't give yours away.

 Your vacation dates. Don't let the world know when you're going to be away from home. Not a good idea.

 Gossip and rumors. That's all they are, so don't be malicious and spread them around as if they are facts.

 Unflattering photos. Your friends won't thank you for broadcasting their bad hair days to the world.

 Rude responses to comments. This is especially true if you don't really know the person whose post you are commenting on. You'll only annoy people and start a huge online fight.

 Private messages. If they're private, keep them private and make sure they only go to the person you intend to read them.

 Chain emails. Don't forward any messages that warn that something nasty will happen to you if you don't pass them on. Something nasty will NOT happen – and if you send them on, you're creating a nuisance for other people.

I know you guys said you didn't want to hear about my health worries any more, but my tongue looks really pink this morning. Am I getting ill?

WHO IS .reading?

Think about what you post online, because you never know who is looking at it. A lot of what you write and do can be retrieved – even if it was a long time ago, or you think you've deleted it.

Thinking ahead

Things that seem funny or cool to put online now might not seem so great if your parents stumble on them. Worse, future employers often check Facebook or Google the name of potential employees to see what they can find.

What can you do?

* Keep your profiles set to private. Check your privacy settings frequently as some sites change them every now and then. Make sure your pictures and posts can only be viewed by yourself and people you have invited to view them.

* Keep your passwords secret and change them regularly. If someone logs on to a site and pretends to be you, they can cause a big problem. Never share your password with anyone, not even your best friend. Use a password that no one will guess – two random words and a number works well.

Yes, even your grandparents may be Googling you...

* Never post inappropriate or suggestive pictures or comments, as these are likely to come back to haunt you. The rule is: if you're not happy for all your classmates, parents, or grandparents to see it, don't post it.

* If you are sent messages that make you feel scared or uncomfortable, do not reply, and report them to an adult. Replying is likely to make the situation worse, and you may end up saying something you regret.

I can't believe my friend posted that!

THE LOW DOWN

Trolling

Internet trolls are people who use their online anonymity to stir up trouble. They purposely leave hurtful and abusive messages or make controversial statements, hoping to start an argument. Trolls like a big audience, so they love blog sites, news sites, discussion forums, and game chat. The only way to deal with trolls is to ignore them, or report them so that an administrator will bar them from posting online.

Beware of trolls!

23

YOU DON'T WANT
anyone TO SEE THAT!

I t's so easy to post online from your computer, camera, or phone that you might find you are doing it without thinking.

A hammer will not delete your Internet history.

STOP!

Almost 40% of Internet users between the ages of 18 and 35 have regretted posting personal information about themselves or about a friend or family member. Most sites have an option to delete a post or photograph, but as soon as something is online and available for everyone to see, it can be saved and reposted by other people – it only takes a matter of seconds to take a screengrab on a phone. Then whatever you posted is out of your control. It could be on the Internet forever, so think before you post.

GIRL TO GIRL

"I posted a mean thing about my friend on a Facebook page. I didn't think I knew anyone else on the page, so no one would see it – but my friend saw it. She knew it was me, because she hadn't told anyone else the thing I'd written about. I deleted the post and apologized. We're friends again, but she doesn't tell me her secrets any more."

"I wrote a pretty offensive comment about a YouTube video when I was in a really bad mood. Now the top comments on the video are all replies to me, telling me what a loser I am. I know I should stop reading them, but I can't seem to!"

THE LOW DOWN

What is spam?

Spam is flooding the net with many copies of the same message, in an attempt to force people to read it. The term came from a Monty Python sketch in which a restaurant kept putting Spam (a canned meat) in its food whether people ordered it or not!

"I was chatting on Facebook, and this boy told me he liked me. So I told him I liked him too – then he told me he had been joking. OMG. I have never been so embarrassed in my life. I hope he doesn't let anyone else see what I wrote!"

25

Cyberbullying

... HOW TO STOP IT!

Unfortunately, there will always be people in the world who are bullies. It's easy to use social networking sites to bully other people or to post hurtful information. You can help to stop it.

Reporting people online is confidential – the person you report will not know it was you. So don't be afraid.

Report it!

If you see anything online that amounts to bullying – either towards yourself or someone else – then you should act to stop it. You can report abuse with the "report" button on social networking sites and the moderator (the person who looks after the site) can then decide to block that information and block the user who posted the comments.

Web sites that host videos, such as YouTube, can take down videos if they are offensive. You can report a video by clicking on "flag content as inappropriate" under the video.

All about you

Cyberbullying

Cyberbullying is the use of technology to harass, threaten, or embarrass another person. It can include:

* A text message, tweet, or status update that is cruel.

* Pretending to be someone online in order to make fun of them.

* Posting photos or personal information about someone online with the intent to upset them.

Sometimes cyberbullying can happen accidentally – for example, a joke might be taken the wrong way. But if someone won't stop joking – or makes the same "jokes" over and over again, the chances are they are doing it on purpose.

GIRL TALK

Real-life advice

Cyberbullying can be easy for someone to do because they feel safe behind a screen. However, if you keep a record of what they have said, you have proof of what has happened.

That video of your brother singing karaoke is wrong, but I guess it's not actually *offensive.*

27

INTERNET slang

There are a lot of words flying around about the Internet and social network sites. Are you Internet savvy? Take this multiple choice quiz, check your answers, and give yourself a point for every one you get right.

1. What is a newbie?
A – someone who's new to something
B – someone who doesn't want to learn
C – someone who is under the age of 14

2. What is app short for?
A – appliance
B – application
C – apple part

3. What's a cyberbully?
A – someone who is cruel to computers
B – someone who plays online action games
C – someone who bullies other people via social networking sites

4. What do you do if you "flame" something?

A – make insulting remarks on a message board or forum

B – rave about how good something is on a message board or forum

C – ignore important messages

5. What is blog short for?

A – Web log

B – beach log

C – Bob's log, after the first person to ever write one

6. What's a troll?

A – a virus that attacks social networking sites

B – a funny joke that gets passed around social networking sites

C – someone who posts rude or irritating comments on social networking sites

7. What is phishing?

A – attempting to obtain personal information via fake emails

B – inviting people to fake events via joke emails

C – advertising vacations via emails

8. What is malware?

A – malicious software that vandalizes your computer or steals your information

B – game software that is out of date

C – expensive software that isn't worth the money

ANSWERS

1. A	5. A
2. B	6. C
3. C	7. A
4. A	8. A

1-3 points

Hmm… you really are a newb. Keep on surfing and before you know it, you'll be teaching others!

4-6 points

You're finding your way through the net without too many tangles. Well done!

7-8 points

You are totally Internet-savvy! Your friends can come to you for advice anytime!

Safety first

Stories from my life

After Sophie's brother made such a fool of me on Facebook, I shut myself in my room and cried. Mom came to ask what was going on. She was really nice about it, and we went on my computer and changed my profile picture back to something normal and deleted the status. We went through all the privacy settings on my Facebook page as well, and I deleted the people whom I had as friends but didn't really know and who had been making mean comments.

But I didn't feel totally better because I knew that everyone still knew and was going to be talking about it at school tomorrow. Mom said I was just going to have to try to laugh about it all tomorrow and act like I found it funny. After all, Sophie's brother was only joking. So, I'm going to try and do that. One thing I know is – I'll never leave my laptop open on Facebook again!

No one will guess my password now!

THE LOW DOWN

The top five most common passwords are...

1. password
2. 123456
3. qwerty
4. letmein
5. 123abc

If your password is one of these, then change it NOW! They are too easy for hackers and other malicious strangers to guess and use to break into your online accounts. A really strong password has eight characters or more with a mixture of letters and numbers. "Welcome" is a bad password. "Well993come" is better – if you can remember it!

My password used to be "neverforget" but, er, I forgot it...

OK, I want you to remove that picture. And that one. Oh, and that one...

TALKING *Point*

Has anyone ever pretended to be you on the Internet, or have you ever done it to someone else? Do you think it was funny or mean?

FRIENDS OR
strangers?

Sometimes, you might enjoy talking to someone online so much that you want to meet up in real life. This could be fine and the start of a great friendship – but there is always a danger that something might go wrong.

Meeting up?

It can be great meeting people online and forming friendships with people interested in the same things. However, do you really know who the person is on the other side of the screen?

You might think you know someone, but all you really know is what they have told you – and this might not be a true picture of who they are.

Unfortunately, being online means you can hide your identity, and people often lie about their name, age, gender, and interests.

Never agree to meet someone from the net and never agree to doing anything alone. If someone you have been chatting to wants to meet up, always talk to a trusted adult who can help you decide if this is safe. Don't put yourself in a dangerous situation.

It could be anyone hiding behind that smiley face...

GIRL TO GIRL

"There's an app on Facebook that shows your top "stalkers," but it's just friends who look at your page a lot. I think it's quite insulting to be called a stalker if you are not, and it should be taken more seriously – because stalking could be a real problem for some people."

"I was chatting to a guy online and he asked for rude pictures. I said no way! It was scary though. I blocked him from my friends list and changed my account to private."

"I heard in the news about a girl who kept getting messages from a really creepy guy who worked in a local store. She reported him, and it turned out he'd been doing it to loads of other girls – some were only 12. It was good that she reported him – it could have turned out badly."

Yakkety YAK

Online chat rooms are great for meeting people with similar interests to you. It's great to chat with people, have discussions, broaden your horizons, and meet new people. Some of the fun can come from the fact that no one knows you.

Online I'm jay_xoxoxo. But in real life I'm Jane.

Chat advice

* Use a separate email account for chat rooms to help keep your regular account safe from hackers.

* Stick to the age guidelines. If a chat room says "Over 18s only," then you should stay away until you are old enough.

* Don't use your real name as your username. Try to pick something neutral and non-identifying (no references to your first name, last name, nickname, town, street, etc.).

* If you find the atmosphere of the chat room stressful, just leave. You don't have to stay there if someone is saying something you find upsetting.

✳ Keep a record of any conversations that seem weird in case you need to report them.

✳ As much as possible, don't open files that you are sent. They may contain a virus.

✳ Be friendly and supportive. Remember that the people you are talking to are real, and you can hurt their feelings even if you can't see their reactions.

TOP FIVE...
rules for chat room chat!

1 DO say hi when you enter the chat room.

2 DON'T give out any personal information such as your name, address, or phone number.

3 DO respect other people in the chat room.

4 DON'T ask lots of questions about how the site works until you've taken a look at the chat room's FAQs.

5 NEVER go on your own to meet someone you have met in a chat room (see pages 32–33). People in chat rooms are not always who they say they are.

35

Seeing things

YOU DON'T WANT TO

Anyone can post things on the Internet anonymously, which means that you might come across things online that you wish you hadn't.

Be smart

* If you see something that you don't like, just close the screen and tell an adult you trust. If you think the content might be illegal, they can help you to report it.

* If someone you are chatting with starts to say things that make you feel uncomfortable, or asks you to do things that you know are wrong, you should save the conversation, then report the person to the administrator of the site.

* Remember, if a friend shows you something you don't want to see on his or her computer, it's okay to say that you don't want to look.

My best friend wants to show me all her vacation photos. Not rude - just dull!

Keeping it real:
What is inappropriate content?

When it comes to knowing what's right and what's wrong, you should trust your instincts. But some types of online content are illegal – end of story. Illegal content includes:

☑ Hateful messages about people's race, nationality, or sexual orientation (for example being gay)

☑ Terrorist-related material

☑ Child abuse images

THE LOW DOWN

What is a meme?

A meme (rhymes with team) is an image, video, phrase, or idea that spreads from one person to another over the Internet. Usually these are inoffensive and funny, such as Lolcats – photos of cats with a caption written in "lolspeak."

Cats show up in loads of Internet memes.

Quiz

HOW IS YOUR NET/LIFE
balance?

Do you spend too much time online? Answer the questions and follow the arrows to find out!

If you're bored, do you turn the computer on before anything else?

YES

NO

START HERE!

Do you check your phone as soon as you wake up?

YES

NO

Do you update your Facebook status regularly more than twice a day?

YES

NO

If you want to tell a friend something, do you text rather than call?

YES

NO

Do you have your phone on the table at dinner?

YES →

NO

Are you often online after 10pm?

YES

NO

YES

Would you interrupt a friend to check a text message?

NO

Do you sometimes upload pictures to Facebook?

YES

NO

YES

Do you check your emails at least once each day?

NO

TURN OFF!

You look after your online identity more than your real one. Turn off for a few hours every day – you might enjoy it!

SWITCHED ON!

You've got the balance right. You're up-to-date with what's happening online, but you have a social life, too !

SWITCHED OFF!

Hmm... you're not into this stuff, right? That's fine, but make sure you're not completely out of the loop!

Boy talk
FROM HIS POINT OF VIEW

Boys use the Internet just as much as girls, but the way they use online technology can be different – and so can their attitude towards social media sites and networking.

Boys vs. girls

One study conducted recently shows quite a difference in the way that teen boys and girls use social media.

TEEN BOYS

* 60% text daily
* 22% have tweeted
* 42% love posting photos

TEEN GIRLS

* 77% text daily
* 33% have tweeted
* 75% love posting photos

In the same study, boys were shown to be less bothered about their online image than girls. They were less worried about feeling left out when seeing photos of their friends online, and a lot less worried about seeing bad photos of themselves.

BOYS SAY...

"I think texts are really easy. I don't always want to get into a long conversation with people, so I use texts to let people know what I'm up to and if I need to arrange anything."

"I never update my Facebook page. My girlfriend gets annoyed with me because she's on there all the time and she wants to know what I'm up to. But I feel like she's trying to keep tabs on me, so I don't do it!"

"My friend once posted a terrible picture of me on Facebook. He offered to take it down afterwards, which was cool of him, but I said I didn't mind, even though I did! Go figure.'"

HEALTHY you!

It's so easy to get online that it's tempting to spend ALL your time online! But that's not always a good thing...

Net/life balance

✳ Studies have shown that the more time young people spend in front of a screen (TV or computer), the more likely it is that their school work deteriorates. Relationships with family and friends can suffer, too. There have been reports of people spending up to seven hours a day on Facebook! If that sounds even a little bit like you, then slow down. There's a whole world out there, and you don't have to access it via a screen.

✳ Also, people sometimes hide their problems behind an online persona by playing online games or visiting social media sites, and that's not always good for your health. It's much better to talk about your problems face-to-face with family or friends.

I'm getting really tired now, just one more status update before bedtime...

Keeping it real:

Turn it off!

If you find yourself compulsively checking your emails and tweets or updating your status many times a day, then take a reality check. Here's what you could do instead:

 Go out with your friends. Go to a café or for a walk and make sure you talk!

 Get some exercise. Go for a bike ride or a swim.

✔ Take time with your family over a meal. People like to chat and catch up with what's going on in each other's lives. Mealtimes are the perfect opportunity.

✔ Read a book. Let your imagination create scenes and characters for you instead of absorbing other people's on-screen ideas and images. Lose yourself in an elaborate story, rather than reading a stream of short messages.

 Catch up with your schoolwork. Do your homework, and make sure you've got all your subjects covered.

✔ Help around the house. Your parents will sing your praises (and might even raise your allowance)!

TALKING *Point*

How much time do you think you spend every day in front of a screen? Add it up and find out for real!

FAQs

Q All my friends have smartphones, but my parents say I can't have one. I feel like I am not part of the group as I can't join in with what they are doing. What can I do?

A *Talk to your parents and find out their reasons. If they think you are not old enough for a smartphone, or if they are worried about the expense, you could offer to get a weekend job or help around the house to show that you are mature enough. But bear in mind that real friends shouldn't make you feel left out just because you don't have a cool phone. Friendship is about enjoying each others' company and interacting face-to-face, in real time, not showing off or communicating via the latest gadgets.*

Q I got a friend request from a girl from my old school. There's no way I want to say yes. But what happens if I see her and she asks me about it?

A *There's no law that says you have to respond to everyone who contacts you online, but it sounds like it would be rude – and potentially awkward – to ignore this girl. Why not send her a private message, telling her you are pleased she contacted you, but that you are keeping your friends list very small at the moment. She may still be annoyed, but it is better than running into her and having to pretend you didn't see her request – nobody ever believes that!*

Q I play online games all the time, but my mom says it's too much and I need to stop. How can I tell if I am getting obsessed?

A *People love playing video games because they are an escape from real life and because they enjoy the challenge. Games can help you build self-esteem, make you feel in control, and are a way to bond with other friends. Some people enjoy video games more than others – and the ones who don't might not understand why the others are having so much fun. Ask your friends to tell you – truthfully – if they think you are playing too much. Signs that you are could include:*

* *The games are affecting your personality or behavior.*
* *You are staying up all night, every night, playing.*
* *You are spending all your money on games.*
* *Your friend doesn't want to play when she comes around, and it makes you mad.*

Q One of the girls at school unfriended me on Facebook, and I don't know why. She's not my best friend, but I still thought we were friends. Why would she do that?

A *The first thing to do is to work out if the girl was really a friend. Sometimes people casually accept friend requests from people they hardly know, just to get their numbers up – then they equally casually unfriend them for no good reason. However, if the girl has a real reason for unfriending you, the best thing to do is to talk to her – in person. You could tell her that you tried to send her a message on Facebook, then realized you weren't friends anymore. Then ask her if it was an accident or if you have upset her, and take it from there.*

Glossary
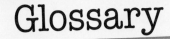

acronym A word formed from the first letters of other words, for example LOL stands for "laughing out loud."

administrator The person responsible for maintaining a Web site.

anonymous A person whose name or identity is unknown.

copyright Laws that regulate the use of the work of a creator, such as an artist or author.

cyberbully Using the Internet or other technology to harm other people in a deliberate or repeated way.

etiquette The rules of polite behavior that are used among members of a group.

forum An online discussion site.

gender Your sex, i.e. male or female.

Google An Internet search engine that provides access to billions of Web pages.

hacker A person who accesses a computer system by breaking into its security system.

harass To make repeated small scale attacks on someone.

malicious Intending to do harm to someone.

persona A character or personality that someone chooses to create.

screengrab An image taken by a camera from another screen.

smartphone A mobile phone with advanced computing capability that can connect to the Internet.

social media The use of computers and mobile devices to communicate with others.

social networking The use of Web sites to communicate with others, by posting messages, photographs, etc.

stalker Someone who displays unwanted and obsessive attention to another person.

trending To be currently popular, for example a topic on Twitter.

virus On a computer, a program that copies itself and spreads from one computer to another, often destroying or corrupting files.

glossary *An alphabetical list of terms or words, with explanations.*

Get help!

There are places to go to if you need more help. The following books and Web sites will give you more information and advice.

Further reading

Bullies, Bigmouths, and So-Called Friends by Jenny Alexander (Hodder 2006)

Cyberbullying (True Books: Guides to Life) by Lucy Raatma (Scholastic 2013)

The Internet for Dummies by John R Levine and Margaret Levine Young (John Wiley and Sons 2011)

Living with the Internet and Online Dangers (Teen's Guides) by Corey Sandler (Checkmark Books 2010)

Netiquette: A Student's Guide to Digital Etiquette (Digital and Information Literacy) by Kathy Furgang (Rosen Central 2011)

Staying Safe on Facebook: A Guide for Teens by Kathryn Rose (CreateSpace 2012)

Web sites

Due to the changing nature of Internet links, Rosen Publishing has developed an online list of Web sites related to the subject of this book. This site is updated regularly. Please use this link to access the list:

http://www.rosenlinks.com/GTALK/Online

Index